Queen Elizabeth II
Monarch of Our Times

Sara Barton-Wood

HODDER

Wayland

© 2001 White-Thomson Publishing Ltd

Produced for Hodder Wayland by
White-Thomson Publishing Ltd
2/3 St Andrew's Place, Lewes, BN7 1UP

Editor: Liz Gogerly
Cover Design: Jan Sterling
Inside Design: Joyce Chester
Picture Research: Shelley Noronha –
    Glass Onion Pictures
Proofreader: Alison Cooper

Cover: Queen Elizabeth II on a walkabout in 1992.
Title: A happy Queen Elizabeth II as she leaves the chapel
at the wedding of her son Prince Edward in June 1999.

Published in Great Britain in 2001 by Hodder Wayland,
an imprint of Hodder Children's Books
This paperback edition published in 2002

British Library Cataloguing in Publication Data
Barton-Wood, Sara
    Queen Elizabeth II: monarch of our times. -
(Famous Lives)
    1. Elizabeth, II, Queen of Great Britain
    2. Queens - Great Britain
    3. Great Britain - History - Elizabeth II, 1952 - I. Title
941'.085'092

ISBN 0 7502 3886 0

Printed in Hong Kong by Wing King Tong

Hodder Children's Books
An division of Hodder Headline Limited
338 Euston Road, London, NW1 3BH

Picture Acknowledgements
The publisher would like to thank the following for giving
permission to use their pictures:
Associated Press 23 (bottom); Camera Press 4, 20, 23
(top), 33, 36, 38, 39, 41, 42, 44/ Stewart Mark 5, 40/
Bassano 6/ Marcus Adams 8, 11/ Cecil Beaton 10, 19/
James Reid 22/ Patrick Lichfield 24, 27, 28/ Godfrey
Argent 25/ Jack Esten 26/ Mark Stewart 29/ Richard
Stonehouse 31/ John Stirling 32/ G. Harvey 35/ Theodore
Wood 37; Corbis (cover); Popperfoto (title page), 7 (top and
bottom), 9, 12 (left and right), 13, 14, 15 (top and
bottom), 16, 17, 18, 21, 30, 43, 45.

Contents

The Making of a Queen

It is Tuesday June 2, 1953 – Coronation Day. The sky is a dreary grey, and light drizzle falls on 30,000 people lining The Mall in London. Millions more, in homes throughout the country, watch on the little black and white screens of their new television sets. Every so often, a cheer goes up as the crowd spots another royal figure or foreign head of state in the procession of carriages.

'The things which I have here before promised, I will perform and keep. So help me God.'
The words the Queen said on her Coronation Day as she laid her hand on the Bible.

The Golden State Coach carries the Queen back to Buckingham Palace after the coronation ceremony. In her hand is the orb, one of the signs that shows she is now a crowned queen.

Just before 11 am, the Golden State Coach leaves Buckingham Palace. Inside is a young woman with an eager face and a radiant smile. It is Elizabeth II on her way to be crowned in Westminster Abbey. The promises she makes in the Abbey that day – to govern fairly and keep faith with her people – will guide her reign as Queen for the rest of her life.

Since that day, almost fifty years have passed. Prime ministers and governments across the world have come and gone. For most people, life is different beyond recognition. But for the Queen, her duties and her beliefs have not changed. This is the story of her life.

Nearly fifty years later the Queen still carries out her royal duties. Here she is talking to people in Tasmania in the year 2000.

5

Birth and Early Life

Princess Elizabeth Alexandra Mary, as she was named, was born in London on 21 April 1926. At the time, nobody imagined that she would ever become queen. Her grandfather was King George V. But her father, the Duke of York, was his second son. Everyone thought that Princess Elizabeth's uncle David, the eldest son and heir to the throne, would become king, marry and have children who would then follow him. Even for royalty, life sometimes has surprises in store!

'(For Elizabeth) other children always had an enormous fascination, like mystic beings from a different world.' Royal governess Marion Crawford speaking about Princess Elizabeth in 1950.

At fourteen months old Princess Elizabeth already had a steady gaze for the camera. Here she is on her mother's knee. Her father stands behind them. On the left are her grandparents, King George V and Queen Mary. On the right are her mother's parents, the Earl and Countess of Strathmore.

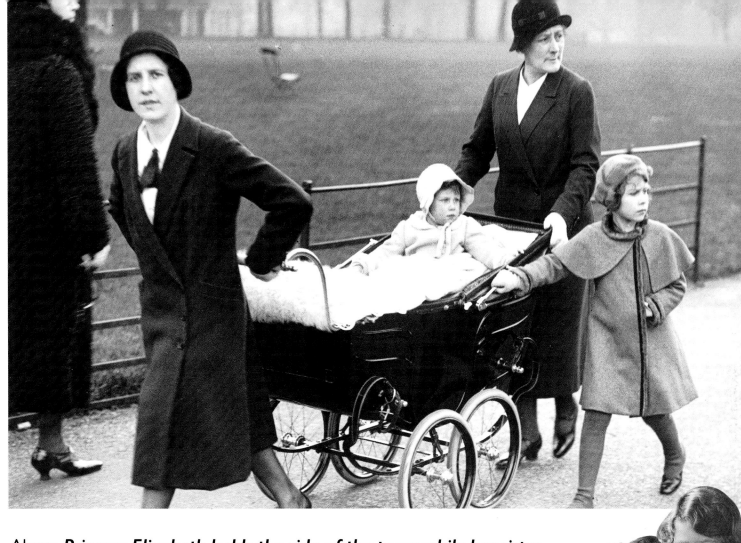

Above **Princess Elizabeth holds the side of the pram while her sister Margaret stays warm and cosy on a walk in the park in 1933. Their nanny pushes from behind while their governess strides out in front.**

Like most rich girls at that time, the young Princess was looked after by a nanny. Clara Knight, known as Alla, was quite strict and did not allow Elizabeth, or her younger sister Margaret, to mix with other children. Instead, she was raised in a very formal way. She was taught to wave politely to the crowds. The pockets of her dress were even sewn up to stop her fidgeting. All this before the age of three! Fortunately, Elizabeth did not rebel against all the discipline.

Right **Elizabeth and Margaret were both very 'good' children. Here they are at the Strathmore home in Scotland in 1932.**

'Us Four'

Elizabeth's father was very close to his family and called them 'Us Four'. They seemed to be such an ideal loving family. Elizabeth's day began with breakfast in the nursery, followed by a visit to her parents' bedroom. She did not normally see her parents again until tea time, when they all played card games like Snap and Happy Families. Then it was bath time, often supervised by her parents.

Elizabeth's mother, the Duchess of York (now the Queen Mother), said that fresh air and dancing were the best sort of education for young girls. Her father thought horse riding was important, but also wanted her to learn neat handwriting. They never sent Elizabeth and Margaret to school, but when Elizabeth was six, a young Scottish teacher called Marion Crawford arrived as governess to educate them at home.

Elizabeth has a loving arm round both her parents, but her eyes are on Margaret to make sure the baby does not play up!

Dogs and horses have always played a large part in the life of the Queen. Here she is with a favourite corgi called Dookie in 1936.

Crawfie, as she was known, taught Elizabeth and Margaret history (of the royal family), poetry, geography (of the British Empire), maths, English, and later on, French. Elizabeth seemed to excel at everything. She especially delighted her grandmother, Queen Mary, who sometimes helped Crawfie in the schoolroom.

All Change at Buckingham Palace

Edward VIII with his girlfriend, Wallis Simpson. They became the Duke and Duchess of Windsor when he gave up the throne and they married and moved to live in France.

In 1936, the royal family suffered a crisis that changed Elizabeth's life for ever. In January, King George V died, and Elizabeth's uncle David became King Edward VIII. David was popular, charming and handsome but not very interested in duty and responsibility. At that time, a king could not marry a divorced person. But David was desperate to marry his American girlfriend, Wallis Simpson, who had twice been divorced. Rather than abandon Wallis, David gave up the throne. Elizabeth's father now took over as King George VI.

King George was a shy man with a bad stammer. He disliked public life and never wanted to be king, but felt that it was his duty to do so. Elizabeth was now ten years old. She sensed her father's unhappiness, but she also realized that she was now next in line to be queen.

Elizabeth's family moved to Buckingham Palace – an exciting place to live, but with drawbacks for a young girl. Elizabeth often had to remind her younger sister Margaret not to point or stare at people wearing funny hats at garden parties in the grounds.

The family were thrust into centre stage when Edward VIII abdicated. This picture was taken at Buckingham Palace shortly after the coronation of King George VI, Elizabeth's father.

War Years

In 1939 the Second World War broke out. When London was heavily bombed by German planes, nowhere was really safe. Even Buckingham Palace was hit nine times. Princesses Elizabeth and Margaret were sent away to live at Windsor Castle. Their parents stayed in London and only saw them at weekends.

King George VI felt very protective towards his children. Elizabeth was now a teenager and wanted to join one of the services fighting the war. Her father refused to allow this. Instead, her war effort consisted of collecting tin foil, rolling bandages and knitting socks. Of all her jobs, knitting was the one she most hated.

Left *A rare photo of Princess Elizabeth taken when she was thirteen, just before war broke out. She won the Challenge Shield at the Children's Annual Swimming Meet at the London Bath Club.*

Below *The Princesses 'knit for victory' in the gardens of Windsor Castle where they spent most of the war. Until they were in their mid-teens, they dressed the same.*

Just before the war ended in 1945, she was finally 'allowed out'. By now aged nineteen, she joined the Auxiliary Territorial Service where she was known as Second Subaltern Elizabeth Windsor. For perhaps the only time in her life, she was able to enjoy mucking in with ordinary people. She became a fast, skilful driver and even learned to use a spanner!

Her Royal Highness Princess Elizabeth doing a really dirty job – changing the wheel of a jeep at an Auxiliary Territorial Service centre.

'Perhaps we were too happy. I keep thinking of those sailors and what Christmas must have been like in their homes.' Elizabeth, in a letter to Marion Crawford after the battleship *Royal Oak* was sunk in 1939.

My Husband and I

When she was just thirteen, Elizabeth met a handsome young naval officer called Prince Philip of Greece, who showed her round the Royal Naval College at Dartmouth. For the young Princess, it was love at first sight, and she never forgot their meeting.

Clearly Philip was just as impressed by Elizabeth. Six years later, the world was at peace again and Elizabeth had grown into a beautiful young woman. Philip, in his black MG sports car, became a regular visitor to Buckingham Palace. They started going out together and quickly fell in love. Privately they agreed to marry. But King George felt they were too young. Elizabeth was still only nineteen and had hardly met any other young men. He insisted that she went with him and the rest of the royal family on a tour of South Africa.

A photo taken to celebrate the engagement of Princess Elizabeth to Prince Philip in 1947. From the left are Princess Elizabeth, Prince Philip, Queen Elizabeth, King George VI and Princess Margaret.

When they returned, Elizabeth and Philip still wanted to marry and their wedding took place in November 1947. Just one year later their first child, Prince Charles, was born.

Above **The newly-weds and family wave to the crowds from Buckingham Palace balcony. A royal wedding was just what everyone needed to cheer them up after the war.**

Left **To make the people even happier, a new royal baby, Prince Charles, was born just one year later. This was the first picture of the young royal family together.**

'I can see you are sublimely happy with Philip, which is right. But don't forget us is the wish of your ever-loving and devoted Papa.'
King George VI in a letter to Elizabeth after her wedding.

Into Mourning

The war years had been a terrible worry for King George, and he never recovered from the strain. He became increasingly moody and bad-tempered and a major operation for lung cancer left him very weak. Princess Elizabeth began to fear for her father's life.

To ease the pressure on the King, Elizabeth and Philip began to take on more and more royal duties. It was in February 1952, while on an official tour of Kenya, East Africa, that they heard the dreaded news that the King had died. Elizabeth was heartbroken. She immediately cancelled the tour and returned home as Queen Elizabeth II.

The sadness in this picture of the Queen in mourning for her father is so strong you can almost feel the ache in her heart. But it was not acceptable in those days to show emotion openly in public.

Three queens in mourning wait for the King's body to arrive at Westminster Hall for the lying-in-state. From the left are Queen Elizabeth II (his daughter), Queen Mary (his mother) and Queen Elizabeth the Queen Mother (his widow).

The British people, like the royal family, were devastated by the King's death. They had grown to love the King for his bravery, his hard work and his kindness throughout the war. But the new Queen could not grieve for long. Though still only twenty-five, she was now in charge at Buckingham Palace. Her mother, newly widowed, had to find another home and it was a time of great strain for everyone.

'My heart is too full for me to say more to you today than that I shall always work as my father did.'
The Queen to her first meeting of the Privy Council, February 1952.

Coronation

A quarter of the world's population took a day off to celebrate the coronation of Queen Elizabeth II in June 1953. After the long years of war, hardships and shortages, at last there was something to celebrate!

TV cameras were still quite a new invention, and at first the Queen refused to let them into Westminster Abbey to broadcast the service. But the people were horrified. They wanted to see their new Queen on the throne with a crown on her head. The public protest persuaded the Queen to change her mind.

The Golden State Coach bears the Queen down to Westminster Abbey on the day of her coronation.

The coronation follows an ancient tradition going back almost 1,200 years. During the ceremony, the Queen swears an oath and has holy oil placed on her forehead by the Archbishop of Canterbury. Then she holds the orb and sceptre while the Archbishop places the crown on her head. It is a moving moment, but an exhausting one – the crown, with its 2,783 diamonds, weighs 1.5 kilograms.

This picture of the Queen on her coronation day was taken by society photographer Cecil Beaton.

'(As we watched from the crowd) one peer dropped his coronet which bounced musically along the pavement. When he bent to pick it up, his sandwiches fell out of his pocket.'
Bystander at the coronation of Elizabeth II in 1953.

Down to Business

As soon as she was crowned, the Queen got down to work. Since then, her daily routine has changed little. She begins work around 9 am by checking her despatch boxes. These contain British government papers for her to read and sign. Often there are messages from Commonwealth leaders, too. The Queen is head of the Commonwealth, an organization of countries that Britain once ruled, and she takes a keen interest in their affairs.

Later, the Queen's private secretary brings in the post and the morning's newspapers. She must be well informed by the time she meets her staff and advisers. After lunch at around 12.30, she might attend a public engagement. This could be anything from opening a new hospital to meeting the leader of a foreign government. The Queen's life may seem glamorous. But in fact it is very hard work, and is often tedious as well as tiring.

The Queen opens her red despatch box as she starts work. She particularly enjoys reading personal letters to her from ordinary people in the United Kingdom and the Commonwealth.

'She's a very quick reader, and quick to spot mistakes.' The Queen's private secretary, Lord Charteris, talking about the Queen.

One of the Queen's official duties every year is the State Opening of Parliament. Here she is on her way to Westminster to reopen Parliament after the summer holidays.

Being queen involves a lot of travel. Sometimes she travels overnight on the Royal Train to meet 'her people' in other parts of Britain. Foreign visits are especially exhausting. Meetings, walkabouts, speeches and dinners can last all day from 7 am until midnight.

On Tour

A very happy family, now with two children, Prince Charles and Princess Anne, enjoy a break at Balmoral in Scotland in 1953.

> **'England's Queen is the world's sweetheart.'**
> Sir Winston Churchill's secretary Jock Colville, January 1953.

In November 1953 the Queen set off with Philip on a tour round the world, visiting every country in the Commonwealth. Everywhere she went, people turned out to wave and cheer. By now the Queen had two children, Prince Charles aged five and Princess Anne aged three. They stayed at home with the Queen Mother – unlike her grandson Prince William who went with his parents on tour to Australia when he was just a few months old.

Left *A traditional Maori greeting in New Zealand is just one of many types of greeting the Queen has experienced on her travels.*

In her years as monarch, the Queen has visited most of the world's countries and shaken thousands of hands. From uniformed officers sporting rows of medals to tribal warriors in loin cloths, she has met all kinds of people. For most, meeting the Queen is an experience they will never forget.

However, attitudes have changed over the years. By 1977, when she repeated the Commonwealth tour in her Silver Jubilee year, the monarchy was not so popular. Many people said that it was stuffy and old-fashioned and some countries no longer wanted to be associated with British royalty.

Right *The Queen often travelled on tour in HMS Britannia.*
This meant that she could invite her hosts back and offer them wonderful hospitality almost as if she was back at home in one of her palaces.

At Home

Buckingham Palace is the Queen's main home. It is not a cosy place to live in as it has about 600 rooms, most of them very large. But it is a good place to receive important visitors from abroad. There are enough people on the staff to make a decent football team called the Royal Household Football Club. And the Palace receives so many letters every day that it has its own post office.

The royal family at Buckingham Palace in 1972. On the right are the Queen and Prince Philip. On the left are Prince Charles, Princess Anne, Prince Andrew and Prince Edward.

More at home in the country than in the city, the Queen rides Benbow, a favourite horse. In the background is Balmoral, her Scottish home.

If she were an ordinary person, the Queen would probably not choose to live in a city. She much prefers country life where she can ride horses and walk her dogs. Every summer she and the rest of the royal family take a six-week holiday at Balmoral, their private home in Scotland. There she enjoys the mountain scenery and lavish picnics spread out on the purple heather.

For Christmas, the Queen goes to Sandringham in Norfolk. Here she can relax and unwind with jigsaw puzzles and Scrabble, her favourite indoor pastimes. Every year she makes a television broadcast on Christmas Day, but this is recorded in advance at Buckingham Palace.

> **'It is no good, I am not a film star.'**
> The Queen, talking about her 1957 Christmas TV broadcast.

25

With the Family

Some people say that Queen Elizabeth has been more successful as a queen than as a mother. She never shows her feelings in public, and greets her children with a handshake rather than a kiss. In private, also, she can be a bit distant with her family. Even close friends have to address her as 'Ma'am'.

The Queen at the wheel of her car with her children Charles and Anne. She likes to take the wheel and is quite happy to drive a Landrover across rough terrain.

As a young mother, the Queen was busy with royal duties, so she asked Prince Philip to take responsibility for the family. Philip was an enthusiastic father. He spent lots of time in the nursery with their four children, Charles, Anne, Andrew and Edward. But he has also been said to bully his children. It was Philip who insisted that Prince Charles should go to his old school, Gordonstoun in Scotland. Charles hated it, but could not appeal to his mother because she would never interfere.

In public, the royal children often praise the Queen and Prince Philip. But in private there are said to be deep divisions in the family. The Queen is unhappy about Prince Charles's failed marriage and his friendship with Camilla Parker-Bowles.

The family just keeps on growing! This picture was taken at Windsor Castle in 1972.

'My parents were marvellous. They would outline all the possibilities, but in the end it was up to you.'
Prince Charles in 1980.

Going Public

In 1968 the Queen took a bold step. She decided to allow BBC cameras into the private life of her family for the first time. The aim was to make a film called *Royal Family*, which would show her family as 'normal' and even fashionable. Prince Charles, then aged twenty-two, was filmed water skiing, and riding a bicycle in a London street. The final shots showed the Queen and her family cooking a barbecue at Balmoral, having fun just like anyone else.

'Most journalists just want the shot where you're seen picking your nose.' Prince Philip to Richard Cawston, the maker of the film *Royal Family*.

Prince Philip and Princess Anne enjoy cooking food over a barbecue in Scotland. This shot is taken from the film **Royal Family.**

The Queen enjoys a break in the Lake District in August 1999. These days the Queen is happy to be photographed in more relaxed poses. Clearly, she also enjoys a joke.

The BBC made a second programme in 1992, called *ER*, filmed over a year of the Queen's life. It showed her at work, at the races and having her portrait painted. This is much more about the Queen herself, rather than her family. It shows her as very good at her job, but with a great sense of humour too.

Should the Queen have allowed these films to be made? They were certainly very popular at the time. But some people say that they opened up the royal family to unnecessary publicity which has been harmful, especially to the children.

Wit and Wisdom

There is nothing like a good wedding to make a person smile! Here the Queen cheats a bit because the guests at the wedding of her son Edward and Sophie Rhys-Jones had been told not to wear hats. But who minds about a few purple feathers?

Nobody likes a good joke more than the Queen. Her sense of humour is famous and she does not like people who cannot laugh at themselves. Some people say that this was why she and Margaret Thatcher, the former prime minister, did not get on well.

Once, it was rumoured that Prince Philip had grown a beard while he was away on a foreign tour. The Queen and all her staff put on false ginger beards to welcome him home. Prince Philip was startled by this strange sight. But the Queen, like everyone else, collapsed in fits of giggles.

'We'll go quietly.'
The Queen commenting on proposals to abolish the monarchy.

The Queen is quite happy to laugh at herself. She even used to enjoy *Spitting Image*, a television programme which made fun of the royal family. But there are limits. Some younger royals, including Princes Andrew and Edward, took part in a TV game show called *It's a Royal Knockout*. They dressed up in silly clothes and played silly games. The Queen did not approve. She thought it made the royal family look ridiculous.

Silver Jubilee

In 1977, the Queen celebrated her Silver Jubilee after 25 years on the throne. Nobody thought that it would be much fun. Britain was not doing well. A huge number of people were unemployed, and the government had very little money to spare for a big public party.

Below **The Silver Jubilee in 1977 was another chance for Britain to show off all the gorgeous trappings of the monarchy. The Golden State Coach is set off by the brilliant red uniform of the footmen.**

'She had a love affair with the country.'
The Queen's private secretary Lord Charteris on the Queen's jubilee year.

Above **The highlight of the Silver Jubilee for the Queen was the chance to meet and talk to so many ordinary people.**

But the Queen's advisers felt that the Jubilee should be celebrated anyway. Despite everything, it was a high point of her reign. All over Britain, people celebrated with street parties. As she toured the country, ordinary people lined the streets to catch sight of her, or tried to give her flowers or shake her hand. Despite all the criticism of the monarchy, most people were still very fond of her as a person. The Queen was rather embarrassed, but also deeply moved.

During her Jubilee year, the Queen even visited Northern Ireland. The violence there between Catholics and Protestants meant that her life might be in danger. Courageously, she insisted on going. She believed that everyone in the United Kingdom had a right to see her.

All the Queen's Horses

The night before she was crowned, the Queen was asked if she was nervous. She replied, 'Yes, but I feel sure my horse will win!' Perhaps she was just being funny. Or maybe she really was more anxious about the next week's horse-race than about her coronation the next day. What the story shows is how much the Queen cares about her horses.

Horses are the Queen's main hobby. She is a skilled horse rider herself, and to relax she loves to go riding 'off the beaten track' on her estates. But she is also an expert on breeding race-horses. At Sandringham and Wolverton in Norfolk she owns studs where her mares are mated to produce foals.

Some people say that the Queen is happier with horses than with people! Here she is making friends with a young foal at Sandringham.

Trooping the Colour is one of the most popular tourist attractions in London during the summer. But the Queen no longer rides with soldiers. She takes the salute from a horse-drawn carriage.

'The Queen is one of the most successful owner-breeders in England, possibly in the world.' Lord Caernarvon, her racing manager, speaking to the author of this book.

The Queen's race-horses have won every important race except the Derby. Probably her most successful horse was Highclere. In 1974, Highclere won important races at Newmarket in England and Chantilly in France, earning her £154,000 in prizes. Blue Print was another famous horse, winning at Ascot in 1999 and at Newmarket in May 2000.

And all the Queen's Men

The Queen's duties include weekly meetings with the British prime minister. Her first prime minister was the famous wartime leader Winston Churchill. Churchill did not take her seriously at first because she was so young. Some people said that he was a little bit in love with her! Since then she has dealt with eight prime ministers, including Margaret Thatcher (the only woman) and Tony Blair.

She is also closely involved with the leaders of the Commonwealth, a group of about fifty countries which Britain once ruled. The Commonwealth is very important to the Queen, and she goes out of her way to meet and support its leaders.

The Queen and Margaret Thatcher were seventy years old in the same year, 1995. Here they are pictured at the former prime minister's seventieth birthday.

The Queen is 'above politics'. This means that she is not allowed to take sides in arguments between politicians of different parties. But she does give advice, based on her long experience of government. She especially enjoyed working with James Callaghan, a Labour prime minister in the 1970s, who amused her with stories about life in parliament.

The Queen and Prince Philip stand on either side of Tony and Cherie Blair outside 10 Downing Street, the official home of the prime minister.

'She thinks they are all rather stupid. Well, perhaps not stupid, but they make mistakes.' A senior royal adviser.

'Annus Horribilis'

Diana and the Queen Mother look in opposite directions. The Queen would have liked everyone in her family to be on friendly terms. Sadly this was not possible.

1992 was a bad year for the Queen. She has always valued family life. But in 1992, her daughter Princess Anne separated from her husband Mark Phillips, and Prince Andrew separated from his wife Sarah Ferguson. Photographs of Sarah with a new boyfriend appeared in the newspapers. Then the marriage of the Prince and Princess of Wales collapsed, and a book called *Diana, Her True Story* was published. The book made the Queen and her family, especially Prince Charles, appear to be very cold, unfeeling people.

But there was worse to come. In November Windsor Castle, the Queen's favourite home, caught fire and was badly damaged. The Queen herself helped to rescue valuable pictures from the flames.

No wonder the Queen described 1992 as her 'annus horribilis' which in Latin means 'horrible year'. In a speech at London's Guildhall, she admitted that she was feeling unhappy. It was a bold thing to say. Normally the king or queen has to pretend that things are going well.

Surveying the damage with a fireman the morning after Windsor Castle caught fire. For the Queen, it was a dreadful end to an awful year.

'1992 is not a year on which I shall look back with undiluted pleasure.' The Queen in a speech at the Guildhall, London.

Death of a Princess

After the horrible year, the Queen probably hoped things would improve. Sadly, the arguments between Prince Charles and Princess Diana got worse. The couple separated and eventually divorced. The Queen was upset for her son and his two children, William and Harry. But she was also worried that the future of the royal family would be damaged by the divorce.

Then, on the morning of 31 August 1997, the world woke to terrible news. Diana and her friend Dodi Fayed had been killed in a car crash in Paris. Britain went into deep shock. Many people travelled to Diana's London home to weep and lay flowers. Astonishingly, the Queen and the rest of the royal family remained in Scotland, on their late summer holiday, showing no sign of mourning!

This picture was taken on the day the Prince and Princess of Wales were divorced in 1996. The Queen hoped that her family life would now become more peaceful.

Diana's coffin was drawn through the streets of London on the day of her funeral so that as many people as possible could say a final farewell to her.

Many people were very upset and angry. It looked as if the Queen was ignoring the grief of the people. Newspaper headlines criticized her for not showing she cared. Television cameras filmed people in a state of shock outside Kensington Palace – but no sign of anyone from the Queen's family. Eventually the Queen travelled to London and, with Prince Philip and Princes William and Harry, went to meet the crowds outside Kensington Palace. That evening she spoke on television, hoping to restore respect and affection for her.

> **'What I say to you now as your Queen and as a grandmother, I say from my heart. Diana was an exceptional and gifted human being. I admired and respected her.'**
> The Queen's broadcast on the eve of Diana's funeral, 6 September 1997.

Keeping up with the Times

Diana's death had a huge impact on the Queen. In truth, she probably did not much like her. But she could see, perhaps for the first time, that Diana was far more popular than anyone else in her family. For the monarchy to survive, it would have to change and become more like the Princess. Even a queen must be in touch with what the people want.

It's not easy being a grandmother and keeping up with new technology. Here the Queen receives a lesson in computer science from children at a primary school.

Old habits die hard – even now the Queen wears gloves to meet the people on a walkabout in Australia in March 2000.

Diana's style was much less formal than that of the rest of the royals. She was openly affectionate in public with her sons, happy to touch people with dreadful diseases like Aids, able to hug people who were sad or desperate. The Queen can never be another Diana. But since Diana's death she has made a real effort to meet more ordinary people instead of lines of public figures wearing strange clothes and gold chains.

The royal family has certainly become more open. The Queen's website is now very popular and is visited by two million 'surfers' every week. When Diana died, 35 million people logged on in one week!

> ***'What the Queen needs is people in daily touch with her who come from outside the court – friendly, natural, loyal, discreet people who know the world outside the palace.'***
> Sir Anthony Jay, 1997.

Life Sentence

Now we are in the twenty-first century, should we still have a queen? It seems that most people in Britain think we should. In Australia, a vote was held in 1999. By a small majority Australians voted to keep the Monarchy.

Edward, Earl of Wessex, and his new wife Sophie, outside St George's Chapel, Windsor, in June 1999. Royal weddings are still popular despite all the problems.

'It's all right for you. You can retire.
I never cease being a Queen.'
The Queen to the Dean of Windsor, 1989.

Having a monarch is certainly expensive – £7.9 million a year to pay for expenses such as staff wages and entertaining visitors. But without a monarch, there would have to be an elected president (like most other countries), who would cost almost as much. The monarchy also attracts many tourists to Britain, and special royal occasions are a wonderful sight.

For the Queen herself, there is no escape. She will probably never give up the throne. In the year 2002, she will celebrate her Golden Jubilee, fifty years on the throne. In all our history, only Queen Victoria has reigned longer. Planning for the celebrations is already under way. Watch your newspapers to see what happens!

The Queen may have another 25 years on the throne. Her own mother is pictured here at Buckingham Palace on her 100th birthday.

Glossary

Affectionate Loving.

Aids Acquired Immune Deficiency Syndrome, a serious incurable disease.

Archbishop of Canterbury The leader of the Church of England.

Auxiliary Territorial Service An organization which helped the army in wartime.

British Empire Countries that were ruled by Britain.

Courageously Bravely.

Criticism Finding fault with something.

Despatch boxes Red boxes containing important or official documents sent from the government to the Queen.

Discreet Someone who does not gossip.

Formal Observing strictly all the rules of proper behaviour.

Governess Someone employed by parents to teach their children privately at home.

Ideal Very good, perfect.

Impact Make a big impression on.

Jubilee The anniversary of an event.

Lung cancer A serious disease, very often leading to death.

Mares Female horses.

Monarchy A government which has a king or queen (a monarch) as its head.

Mourning Expressing grief because someone has died.

Nursery A room where very young children are cared for.

Orb A golden ball set with jewels with a cross on the top.

Sceptre A golden rod set with jewels.

Second Subaltern A young soldier of low rank.

Stuffy Not fresh or interesting.

Tradition How things have been done for many years.

Undiluted Strong.

Walkabout When a famous person goes on foot to meet ordinary people in the crowd.

Further Information

Books to Read

Jokes to tell the Queen by Caroline Plaisted (Bloomsbury Children's Books, 1996)

Royal Children by Ingrid Seward (Harper Collins, 1993)

The Queen Mother by Richard and Sara Wood (Hodder Wayland, 2000)

Royal Websites

The British Monarchy – official website: www.royal.gov.uk

The Royal Collection – royal paintings and homes www.the-royal-collection.org.uk

Places to Visit

Buckingham Palace, London SW1A 1AA. Tel: 020 7839137. The Queen's London home. State rooms and galleries open.

Sandringham House, Sandringham, Norfolk. Tel: 01553 772675. The private family home in Norfolk, open April to October except when the Queen is there.

Windsor Castle, Windsor, Berkshire, SL4 1NJ. Tel: 01753 869898. The royal family's main private home near London.

Holyrood House, Edinburgh EH2 2QP, Scotland. Tel: 0131 556 1096. The official home of the royal family when they are visiting Scotland.

Date Chart

1926 Born in Bruton Street, London.

1928 Sister Margaret Rose born.

1930 Governess Marion Crawford arrives.

1935 Grandfather King George V dies.

1936 Uncle David, King Edward VIII, abdicates. Elizabeth and her family move to live at Buckingham Palace.

1937 Father is crowned King George VI.

1939 Meets Prince Philip for first time. Second World War begins.

1940 Elizabeth and Margaret move to live at Windsor Castle.

1945 Second World War ends.

1946 Privately agrees to marry Prince Philip. Tours Southern Africa.

1947 Marries Prince Philip.

1948 First child, Prince Charles, is born.

1950 Second child, Princess Anne, is born.

1952 Father, King George VI, dies.

1953 Crowned Queen Elizabeth II.

1953–4 Grand tour of the Commonwealth.

1960 Third child, Prince Andrew, is born.

1964 Fourth child, Prince Edward, is born.

1968 Film *Royal Family* is made.

1969 Investiture of Prince Charles as Prince of Wales.

1977 Silver Jubilee. Second grand tour of the Commonwealth.

1981 Wedding of Prince Charles and Lady Diana Spencer.

1982 Birth of grandson Prince William, in line to the throne.

1984 Birth of grandson Prince Harry, William's younger brother.

1992 The film *ER* is made. 'Annus Horribilis' – the marriages of Charles, Anne and Andrew break down and Windsor Castle is badly damaged by fire.

1993 The Queen and Prince Charles agree to pay income tax.

1996 The Prince and Princess of Wales divorce.

1997 Princess Diana is killed in a car crash.

1999 Referendum in Australia retains Queen by a small majority.

August 4 2000 Sends congratulations to her mother on reaching 100.

Index

Page numbers in **bold** refer to pictures as well as text.